This
Little
Book
OF
Offerings

High Vibe Transmissions,
Practices and Meditations

KARINE WASCHER

This Little Book of Offerings

© 2021 Karine Wascher

ISBN PRINT 978-1-09837-331-3 | ISBN eBOOK 978-1-09837-332-0

Dedicated to
You

CONTENTS

INTRODUCTION

Dear One,

This book of offerings is my gift to you

Each message vibrates with an infusion of Light

Every word is encoded with the frequency of love

Welcome these energetic transmissions in the center of your heart

And in every living expression of your embodied soul.

November 18, 2020. Upon waking up, I received a telepathic message. The voice speaking to me was male and held a sense of urgency: "It's now time to write *The* book". My first reaction was astonishment. Who was this voice and what was he referring to? What could I possibly write about? I felt denial. There would be no book. Period. Reading my thoughts, he replied: "The messages will come. We are here". Clearly, he was not about to give up easily. And so began my journey.

During the process of writing this book, I sensed the presence of majestic Light Beings guiding me. They are ancient and cosmic at the same time, merging past and future wisdom into the timeless now. Every page resonates with their essence. The voice that spoke to me was from this group.

The Light Beings guided me with the content of this book. Do not be fooled by the simplicity of the offerings you are about to read. Simplicity holds clarity and truth. It allows you to integrate each transmission with your emotional intelligence. Each message resonates with a unique vibrational quality to alchemize thoughts into reality. The group of Light Beings is clear about this.

This Little Book of Offerings

Each offering was first handwritten. This is part of my creative process. It is a conduit for my intuition. I've also included dedicated meditations and practices in every chapter for you.

Humankind is now entering a new quantum paradigm. The planetary shift is happening now. Ascension technology within us will be activated once we unlock the codes of our junk DNA. The word "junk" is a cover up for highly advanced technology hidden in plain sight. I love to think of DNA as an acronym for Divine Natural Ascension. The exciting news is that you hold the keys to this activation. With gratitude for your Light, I honor you with Love.

Karine

BREATH

A Blessing....

Invite the breath in.

Notice the inhale.

Feel your lungs embracing prana.

Delight in the subtle pause

at the top of the inhale.

Observe the exhale.

Take refuge in the stillness

at the bottom of the exhale.

Sit with yourself.

Sit with

Your Self.

Sit with all of you, the lost child, the broken soul, the wounded warrior

The chaos and the truth that beg for attention

Sit with all of it, for here lives the teacher.

Ride the wave of your breath.

Life beckons.

Breath awareness is a radical act of presence. It settles us into the now, the full expression of your essence. Here, there is no past and no future. Only this moment, filled with Prana. Presence is medicine. You are the Alchemist, the Shaman, the Goddess and the Ascended Master.

Follow the path of your breath and drop into your body. What do you sense? Is your breath expansive? Is it contained? Are you breathing predominantly through one nostril? Which one? Do you notice any movement in your belly and your ribs? Observe sensations and thoughts without judgement.

Our feelings affect the quality of our breath. Anger, sadness, fear and anxiety change its flow and lower our oxygen intake. The breath can become shallow and staggered. The opposite is also true. You can shift your emotional state simply by practicing mindful breathing. Here is a simple exercise. Take 20 steady breaths. Focus your attention on the fullness of each inhale and the release of each exhale. Notice if your overall energy begins to shift. Repeat this exercise and extend the length of each breath without forcing. Take a moment to compare how you felt when you started and how you feel now.

Breath awareness is a wonderful gateway to meditation. I encourage you to dedicate a sacred space in your home for a daily breath and meditation practice. It can be as simple as a meditation pillow or chair in the corner of a room. This is your personal sanctuary. By returning to this space regularly, you imprint it with your energy. Regularity amplifies the resonance of your practice. You may be inspired to add meaningful objects such as crystals, art, plants and books. You may want to include rituals like prayers, mantras and candle lighting. What matters is your intention and comfort.

MEDITATION FOR THE HEART

Settle comfortably into your sacred space. If you want, include rituals to set the tone of your meditation. Begin observing your inhales and your exhales. Can you lengthen both without force? Breath should flow naturally. Count 10 breaths.

Drop deeper into your body. Befriend stillness. Become the Observer. Feel your energy shifting. Notice the subtle movements of your body in conversation with your life force. Welcome the specialness of this moment and its spaciousness.

Drop further into your energetic heart. Let your intuition guide you to this heart space. Sense its presence. Bear witness to your high emotional intelligence, the technology of higher dimensions. Remain present.

Listen to your heart. Does it have a message for you? You may even want to place your right palm over your heart and feel it beating. What is coming up for you in this moment? Listen some more. Become inquisitive. The heart communicates in its own language. Tune in to it. Are there words, colors, symbols, shapes, feelings or thoughts coming up for you to notice? Be honest, truthful and patient. If you feel nothing, that is what you are meant to experience in this moment. Trust yourself. There is no wrong way to do this meditation. Keep breathing, keep listening.

Now drop down further. Move in closer to witness your inner heart. This is the most intimate part of your heart. Start a dialog with it. Trust its intelligence. What does it wish to share with you? What are you receiving? What do you feel?

Remain in this meditation for however long you wish. Know that insights may come through after you're done.

When you are ready to seal your meditation, express gratitude. Thank your heart for its loving messages.

PRACTICE JOURNALING

As you emerge from your meditation and return to your 3D reality, start journaling. This is a wonderful way to awaken your empathic gifts and accelerate your intuition.

YOUR VOICE

Go ahead sweet soul

Speak your Truth.

Now listen

To the silence that follows.

Your voice is your soul's microphone. Spoken words contain encoded frequencies which transmit unique vibrational notes. These energy forms reflect back similar emotions and thoughts into your plasma field. What you project mirrors back to you. You hold this power. Voice is associated to the throat chakra which governs your capacity to express yourself and to listen. Become more aware of your voice and what you are projecting out into the world. Pay special attention to its volume, tone, inflection and the words you use.

Our inner voice reflects the intimate dialog we have with ourselves. It colors the internal landscape of our soul journey. Your words influence your thoughts and emotions. For example, if your internal dialog tends to be judgmental, notice how you feel when you are in that vibration? One of my favorite yogic teachings is the practice of non-harming, also known as ahimsa. This is associated to how we treat ourselves and others both in action and in thought. Many of us unconsciously carry generations of programmed behaviors which influence our internal dialog. Now is the time to recognize negative patterning and release it. Now is the time to shift the narrative and shine your light out into the world.

My mother lost both her parents at a very young age. She was 8 years old when her father died, one year after her mother's passing. She was separated from her brothers and sisters and sent to live with her aunt. Needless to say, she experienced a lot of trauma. One of her survival mechanisms was to be non-confrontational. For many years, I unconsciously did the same. I avoided challenging conversations and situations even when it meant holding back my true feelings. I was a "people pleaser". This pattern also stemmed from a deep seated fear of rejection. When I was born, my aunt who lived in another city took me in for a few months to help my parents who struggled financially. I was too young to remember anything however I often wonder if it impacted me in any way. Being separated from my parents must have left an indelible mark on me. It's taken me years to voice my truth, to be comfortable with the discomfort of perceived rejection. Ultimately, I must take full responsibility for my role in how I interpret events which create comfort. In other words, what stories have I unconsciously told myself? What filters do I apply to narratives? Through the practice of awareness and compassion, I'm learning to shift these narratives. Do I ever revert back to old patterns? Absolutely! However, I can now bear witness to this behavior and transition to a state of awareness and compassion. My inner child is heard.

Your voice is the expression of your Truth. Being honest with yourself is a practice that complements the path of Ahimsa. It invites you to start seeing your life for what it really is, a field of opportunity. Be curious. When you start peeling the layers of deep programming and long held beliefs, you embark on a course correcting journey of discovery. You begin to dissolve the fears that have held you captive. You release survival mechanisms that no longer serve your highest good. That's why this process can feel uncharted, uncomfortable and also filled with great insight. The more you reveal, the more is presented in perfect synchronicity. You meet your inner child. You face your wounded self. For many who unconsciously carry ancestral wounds and traumas, this process takes time. Recognize the important role of your survival skills and do not dismiss them lightly. They've played a vital part in your journey.

Start paying attention to how you vocalize your truth. Be kind to yourself even when you are calling yourself out. I believe this is the work of years and perhaps even lifetimes. The universe constantly presents us with opportunities for growth. It has your back. Reconsider illness, addiction, difficult life experiences and relationships as master teachers. View joy, love, happiness and peace as frequency accelerators.

This is a time of heightened awareness on our planet. We sense a massive shift in consciousness and the emergence of a new paradigm. We are raising our vibration and moving into higher dimensions. This transformation is messy yet necessary. How are you experiencing it? How are you using your voice to speak the new language of love and light?

Our cosmic family is very present, helping us navigate this incredible earth wide event. We are moving into a new expression of our soul blueprint by activating dormant DNA strands. The benevolent higher dimensional beings honor your free will. They offer guidance when you call upon them in prayer and meditation. They have been through this themselves in their evolutionary timeline. Simply ask and listen with your heart. Your voice will be heard. Of this I am unequivocally certain.

PRACTICE INTERNAL LISTENING

Dedicate a day to silence and stillness. If you need to speak, keep it to a minimum to remain focused. View this time as a gift of self-care, a mini retreat and a day dedicated to attuning your throat chakra.

Avoid external stimuli such as your cell phone, computer, television, social media, gatherings and unnecessary conversations. Throughout the day, notice your internal dialog. How do you communicate with yourself? What is your choice of words? Are you compassionate, supportive, curious, loving, happy, judgmental, anxious, fearful? Perhaps even a blend of all of these. What comes up for you when you give yourself this undivided attention? Does it feel uncomfortable? You may experience a range of emotions throughout the day. If you are inspired to extend this practice beyond one day, explore that message.

This is a great practice to clear, cleanse and recalibrate your energy. You can repeat it as often as you like. Each experience will open portals to new insights.

Over the past year, I have integrated silence and stillness into my daily life in a very intentional way. This is the art of bearing witness and being present to what is. I've become much more attuned to my internal landscape. In silence, It's all there.

You can layer this practice with "pray-meditating". Use your inner voice to ask for help, healing and guidance in prayer. Be specific. Broadcast this into the quantum field. Remain present. Then tune into your heart and listen. You are in conversation with Source. Notice what presents itself. Trust the transmission. Activate the technology of miracles.

PRACTICE INTUITIVE LISTENING

This experience encourages you to enhance your intuitive listening skills.

Listen to someone's voice and notice: what words are used, are sentences fully formed or broken, are there pauses, does the voice halter. Notice the volume and tone of the voice. Is this person speaking quickly, slowly, deliberately, confidently or hesitantly? What emotions are being projected energetically?

Begin to develop a heightened awareness of the non-verbal messages being communicated. What underlying themes are you picking up? Do you sense happiness, sadness, anxiety, fear or any other emotion in the texture of their voice? Notice how you receive this information. Observe sensations in your own body during this process. Your innate intelligence will communicate intuitively with you through your senses.

MEDITATION TO COMMUNICATE WITH YOUR GUIDES

Settle comfortably into your sacred space. Make sure that you are undisturbed for the duration of the meditation. Begin breathing mindfully. Gently slow down your inhales and extend your exhales without force. Count 10 breaths. Set an intention that only energies of Light and Love are welcome.

Shift your awareness to your body and feel it relaxing deeply. In your mind's eye, visualize yourself lying down in the center of a beautiful forest. You feel supported by the earth below you. Release any tension in your shoulders, neck and the back of your head. Surrender to the loving embrace of Mother Earth. Release your tongue from the roof of your mouth and let out a big internal sigh of relief. There is nothing to do. Simply rest in the perfection of this moment.

Notice the sun's warm rays on your face. Delight in the sounds of birds chirping as they welcome you to your sanctuary. Listen to the wind in the trees and feel the breeze caressing your skin. Smell the earth's fragrant gifts: the flowers, trees and plants. You've come here to rest and meet your guides.

Begin to feel a soft and loving energy in the air around you. Sense the sacred presence of your spirit guides. They love you unconditionally. They are always with you. Welcome their presence with your heart. Take the time to notice their appearance. They are here in loving presence. Perhaps they are angels, ancestors, ascended masters, spirit animals, galactic beings, fairies or other beings. Bathe in this gift. Maybe it's just one guide.

Using your telepathic voice, start a conversation with your guides. Ask for guidance on anything you wish. Add the following words to your inquiry: "What is in my highest good? What am I here to learn? If you prefer to receive general guidance without asking a question, share this intention with them. Allow your guides the time to respond in their own way. They may communicate through felt sensations, images, sounds, symbols, words, colors, emotions or thoughts.

Repeat your question. This is a wonderful way to delve deeper into your inquiry. If you want more clarity, ask for it as well.

Deepen your breath and begin to raise your energy to a new plane of awareness. In your mind's eye, see yourself rising above the forest. Invite your guides to join you. Feel lighter.

You are now connecting to Source, a quantum space of timeless knowledge. Your guides are with you. Have a felt sense of this limitless field of wisdom. Repeat the same question to Source. and add: "What is in my highest good? What am I here to learn?" Welcome what comes through.

Receive insights.

Thank Source. Thank your guides.

Begin to shift your awareness back to your breath. Feel your physical body resting. Take 10 comfortable breaths.

If you are lying down, roll over gently to your right side and rest here for however long you wish. When you are ready, come up to a seated position and join your palms to seal your meditation with gratitude.

Over the next few days, notice any further downloads and insights.

JOURNAL YOUR IMPRESSIONS

Write down your impressions of this meditation. Use the following questions as inspiration for journaling.

What was the felt sense of this meditation?

What part of it resonated with you? Describe the experience.

Describe your guide(s)?

How did they communicate with you?

What messages and insights did you receive from your guide(s)?

What messages and insights did you receive from Source?

How can you integrate these loving transmissions into your daily life?

TADASANA

Stand in your Power

Barefoot.

Earth below you

Sky above.

Stand in your Sovereignty

Embraced by the elements.

Channel the strength of the Sacred Mountain

Let her song heal your wounded soul.

Here she rises

Weather beaten by the passage of time

Resilient

Majestic

Present

Rooted.

Breathe in her wisdom.

Welcome the frequency of Sacred Mountain medicine

Tadasana, also known as Mountain Pose in yoga, is the central gesture of the yogic practice. It invokes in us a divine connection to the living Earth. We are honored guests of her majestic offerings. Stand tall with both feet firmly rooted. Draw your shoulders towards each other and soften your gaze. Stand your ground with a radiant heart, anointed by earth's blessings. You are the embodiment of all that is, a vessel of Light. Know this without the shadow of a doubt. You are Truth in its purest expression. And so it is.

We all carry the oracle of sacred mountain within our unique expression. We navigate life's experiences by shapeshifting to adapt and evolve. We remain present, at times broken and lost. A deep "inner-standing" of life's impermanence permeates this dance.

MEDITATION ON THE ELEMENTS
Experience the presence of Mother Earth within you.

Lie down on a comfortable surface. Begin breathing slowly. Take 10 deep mindful breaths. Become aware of your body resting. Drop into stillness.

Shift your awareness to the earth's loving presence. In your mind's eye, visualize her fertile soil. Recognize the solid nature of your physical body; your bones, muscles, tendons, ligaments, nails, hair and skin. Now acknowledge the solid nature of the earth; her mountains, trees, soil, valleys, stones and plants. Immerse yourself in her physical expression.

Shift your awareness to the fluids in your body. Visualize your blood delivering nutrients and oxygen to every cell in your body. You are fluid by nature. In your mind's eye, see the earth's waters that nourish you; the streams, brooks, rivers, lakes and oceans. Envision the rain and dew that drench the soil. Immerse yourself in this connection.

Breathe deeply and begin to notice your internal heat. Visualize the sun's warming rays. Encourage your inner light to radiate out like the sun's encoded beams. Feel your creative power.

Observe the natural movement of your breath. Notice how the muscles between your ribs expand and contract with every breath. Welcome oxygen with every inhale and release stagnant energy with every exhale.

Appreciate the air that fills the space all around you. Air within and air without. Through the portal of your own heart, become light.

Cultivate a deep sense of peace. Earth's consciousness is manifested in you. Her soil, her waters, her fire and her air reflected in your unique expression.

Remain in this meditation for however long you wish. When you are ready, invite tiny movements in your fingers and toes. Roll onto your right side and rest. Gently come up to a seated position and join your palms together to seal this meditation. Bow down towards the light in your heart and bless it.

TADASANA MORNING PRACTICE

Practice mindful standing to welcome a new day and cultivate the art of presence, the gift of now.

Stand barefoot in Tadasana, Sacred Mountain Pose.

Notice the soles of your feet making contact with the earth.

Notice your breath.

Breathe in deeply and invite your spine to lengthen by gently drawing in and engaging your belly to retain Prana.

Exhale completely and feel expansive.

Inhale all the way up to the crown of your head from the soles of your feet. Follow the energetic pathway of your breath flowing up your body, enlivening and energizing you.

Exhale completely. Encourage your shoulders to draw towards each other. Your heart and lungs expand. Turn your palms outward in a gesture of receptivity. Feel the life force animating your fingertips.

Stand in the full expression of Tadasana for 1 minute or more.

This Little Book of Offerings

Be fully conscious of your entire being. Present in the now.

You are the mountain, the warrior, the survivor, the lover, the guide, the phoenix. You are all of it in perfect synchronicity. You are timeless.

INTUITION

You've got a superpower. It's called your intuition. This is your innate capacity to access universal consciousness, a state of absolute "Knowing". Every human is blessed with this power. It is our divine right. Our degree of connection to universal Truth varies depending on the veils that shield us from Light. On the following pages, I'll share 6 steps to help you activate and accelerate your intuition. These steps are intended to build a solid foundation for your journey.

Before we delve into them, I invite you to contemplate your intention. Why are you are interested in enhancing your intuition? This is an important question. The following exercise will help you explore this inquiry and create an energetic container for your intuitive exploration.

INQUIRY INTO YOUR INTENTION

Review the following list of suggested words. Select the ones that resonate with your desire. Write them down. Feel free to add your own words to this list.

Guidance

Clarity

Inspiration

Healing

Spiritual growth

Alignment with my higher self

Creativity

Transformation

Connection with light beings

Harmony

Joy

Peace

Help others/be of service to humanity

Focus

Truth

Wisdom

Higher realms

Manifestation

Release Past Trauma

Seal this inquiry with gratitude when you are done. You may be called to journal and further explore insights. Now you are ready to dive into the 6 steps to activating your intuition.

THE 6 STEPS TO ACTIVATING & ACCELERATING YOUR INTUITION

STEP 1: CLEAR YOUR ENERGY FIELD & RAISE YOUR VIBRATION

Clearing and cleansing your energy field is fundamental to establishing a healthy foundation for your intuitive skills. Ideally, you're doing this on a daily basis. There are three foundational pillars associated to this process. These pillars are like the roots of a tree, they ground you.

1. The physical pillar

2. The emotional pillar

3. The spiritual pillar

The first pillar is your physical body. It acts as an antenna for both sending and receiving signals. Your physical body's health impacts your subtle energy. Your goal is to sustain a vibrant body. That's why it's recommended to reduce or eliminate toxins from your diet. Increase your intake of pure water to flush out waste. Water is a wonderful cleansing agent. Limit your consumption of meat, dairy, sugar, processed foods, alcohol, stimulants, and drugs. If you consume any of these, it doesn't mean that you can't be intuitive. It's just easier to hold the higher frequencies of light when your body is uncontaminated. A healthy physical expression supports a clear conduit for information. Everyone's experience is different. Remember that judging others' lifestyle choices is a distortion of your personal power and a distraction. If you decide to embark on a physical cleanse, consider getting support and guidance. Consult with specialists if necessary and be compassionate with yourself during the cleanse.

Your body needs to move every day. Walk, run, dance, do yoga, cycle, swim, play outdoors, even climb a tree. Just move! If you are close to nature, get out and connect with the earth's energy. This is absolutely vital for maintaining a vibrant and healthy vessel. It also strengthens your immune system. I've noticed that if I don't do some form of daily movement, my energy shifts and I don't feel as bright and connected.

Lastly, your physical senses constantly receive and transmit information to your heart center. There are more neurons in your heart than in your mind. That's why we call it emotional intelligence. Pay special attention to disruptive influences such as your cell phone, social media, television, entertainment, conversations, people's energy and even physical locations. Notice what you are allowing into your sacred temple through your senses. Trust what you feel and listen to the messages your body sends you. Oftentimes, your body will feel drained and sluggish as a result. If your energy feels contaminated, reclaim your power and remove yourself from these low vibrational influences. When I sense an energy drain, I try to address it immediately. If that's not possible, I ground myself and refocus my attention within.

The second pillar is the emotional/mental one. As you become more awakened, you begin to notice situations, relationships and events in your life that either raise or lower your frequency. As you accelerate your intuitive skills, you become highly sensitive and more discerning. You are tuned in to subtle energy and experience life from the innate intelligence of your heart center. Emotions create feelings and this is how we project our plasma into the multiverse. Now is the time to reevaluate old habits, thoughts and relationships that no longer serve you. In my personal experience, I've had to address certain relationships because I was no longer showing up in an authentic way. In some cases, the relationships matured and became much healthier after I took responsibility for my truth.

The third pillar is the spiritual one. This is your relationship to Source. In many ways it's what anchors your multi-dimensional transformation. Your spiritual practices are the gateway to inner higher dimensions where intuition resides. Your emotional self is essential in accessing these realms. Meditation, prayer, mindfulness, and intention setting can help you navigate this journey safely and shield you from lower vibrations. It's important to remain grounded and discerning.

We just reviewed the three fundamental pillars associated to clearing your energy and raising your vibration: the physical, the emotional/mental and the spiritual. Establish regular practices to strengthen and support them. In turn, they will strengthen and support you.

STEP 2. ESTABLISH STRUCTURE & RITUAL

The primary benefit of establishing structure on your intuitive journey is to sustain regularity. This intensifies the resonance of your energy field and amplifies your intuitive skills. It's like strengthening muscles with a regular exercise program. Your intuition intensifies and you become more tuned in to Source. Begin by dedicating a sacred space in your home. This is your personal sanctuary. Consider setting up an altar with meaningful offerings that are dear to you such as crystals, candles, plants, art and unique objects. You may even want to add sound and diffuse essential oils. Think of this space as a mini retreat for your heart and soul, a place to regenerate and reconnect through meditation.

Meditation is the art of finding stillness and observing your breath for however long you wish. The stillness might be challenging because our minds are so active. And that's ok. Welcome the internal chatter and notice your thoughts. Acknowledge them with loving detachment. By acknowledging your thoughts, you reclaim your power. Give them the attention they want then encourage them to drift away. Focus your energy and intention on remaining present. You are the Observer.

There are many styles of meditation and ways to meditate. For some, moving meditations are easier than sitting in stillness. For others, sitting in contemplation is more meaningful. Creating art, going for walks, playing music, running, gardening and dancing are just a few examples of how you can access a state of inner peace and connection to your higher self. Be curious and explore what meditation means to you. Try different forms of meditation. See what resonates with you.

In recent years, I've switched up my meditation practice by intentionally extending its resonance beyond the time I'm sitting. I experience meditation as a fluid state of awareness rather than a timed practice. In other words, its energy is infused into every moment. This allows me to navigate the day from a higher frequency. Not every day is perfect. If I'm feeling off, I try to observe what is arising. If I'm sad for example, my practice invites me to experience the sadness as an integral part of my meditative state. Can I be fully present to the full spectrum emotions that turn up and still remain centered. That's not easy. There are challenging moments. Notice how I am judging my experience. Why do I expect my experience to be filled with ease? What am I clinging to here? This inquiry invites me to observe judgement within myself and to consider loving detachment. Ultimately, my goal is to be compassionate with myself and to view the experience simply as what it is, an experience. I've noticed that this approach helps me access my truth in the generous present.

Once you've created your sacred space, think about including rituals to accelerate your connection to Source. I personally enjoy lighting a candle, burning palo santo and playing soft music when I meditate. This helps me transition to another dimension. If you are not drawn to rituals, honor your intuition.

STEP 3: LISTEN INTUITIVELY

We delved into intuitive listening in the previous chapter as a means of enhancing your natural gift. This is a practice of allowing yourself to trust what you tune in to by going within. All the answers are within you. Universal truth resides in your heart and soul, the seat of feeling, imagination and insight. Intuition is 100% feeling.

Your mind is control central. Like a busy airport control tower, it oversees the incoming and outgoing traffic of your thoughts and actions. It plays a vital and necessary role in keeping you safe and healthy. It helps you function and thrive in your 3D reality. Your objective is to expand your intuition without dismissing your mind. We want the mind and the heart to befriend one another.

The mind loves to hold onto power. It wants to be in the driver's seat. One way it does this is by creating narratives which can cast doubts on your feelings. Your ego may voice thoughts like: it's your imagination, you're making it all up, it's not real, you're crazy, there's no scientific evidence for this stuff, where's the proof, etc. When this happens, remind yourself that this is in fact your ego trying to reclaim the driver's wheel. Rather than compete with your ego for control, engage it in a loving dialog. You are in control, not your ego.

In my work as an energy intuitive, I still experience self-doubt which shows up as anxiety and self-judgement. This is my ego asserting itself. If I ignore it, it creates more disruption. I observe my ego's need for control then return my attention to my heart's high intelligence. If I doubt the messages I am receiving, I center myself and stay focused.

One example of this is an incident that occurred with a client named Ann* (name has been changed) during an intuitive energy session. I began with an intuitive body scan and reiki to ground energy and call in Beings of Light. Typically, if the energy is clear I sense lightness. On the other hand, if there is an area to address, the energy can feel dense. My palms feel a magnetic pull. This is how I start receiving information.

As I began working with Ann, my palms paused above her lower belly. I felt a dense energy. I then heard a voice ask: "Where is he?". My first reaction was to dismiss it. I was reluctant to let it disrupt Ann's session. My ego was showing up and creating self-doubt. When ego enters the picture, the energy shifts. After taking a few centering breaths to return to my heart center, I asked Ann if it would be ok to share this message. Upon hearing the question, Ann began crying. She had lost a stillborn son a few years ago after a series of miscarriages. This had devastated her. Although her family and community had supported her grieving process, they encouraged her to move on after a year. She still grieved deeply and carried this pain in her lower belly. During the two hour session, her son came through. He wanted her to know that she didn't have to "move on". In fact, his spirit was right by her side. She realized that she could embrace his beautiful soul. This was a watershed moment for her. A profound healing had taken place.

The voice that spoke to me at the beginning of the session facilitated Ann's healing experience. My self-doubt held it back at first. By releasing my ego's attachment to control, I was able to get out of my own way and entrust the process to Source.

SUBTLE ENERGY PRACTICE

The following practice will help you sense subtle energy and enhance your intuition. You'll need a partner. Repeat this exercise as often as you wish with different people to sharpen your skills.

Sit comfortably face to face with your partner. Ground yourselves by taking 10 deep mindful breaths together. You can close your eyes or gaze at each other. Set an intention to welcome messages of light and love. Your friend's role is simply to sit in stillness and remain present.

Begin to sense your own personal energy field. This is the space around you which extends approximately eight feet outwards in all directions. Trust whatever is arising. Stay here for as long as you wish.

Now shift your awareness to your partner's energy field. Scan their plasma field intuitively. If you need to move your palms around their space, ask for permission first. Are there areas that feel light and clear? Are there areas that feel dense? What do you sense, feel, smell and see? What sensations arise when you pay attention to one area in particular? Trust whatever comes up. This is your intuition picking up information. Don't rush, be patient and open to the process. If you are drawn to deepen your inquiry, do so by remaining in one spot. Oftentimes, more comes up for attention. Remember that self-doubt and self-judgement are your ego blocking your intuitive intelligence.

When you are ready to move to the next stage, shift your attention back to your breath. Begin to further deepen your awareness of your partner's energetic space. Breathe deeply as you shift into this new dimension. You are now in a timeless space where the past, present and future are merged as one. A place where you can dialog with multiverse frequencies. What are you now sensing about your friend? Remember to trust your intuition. If you receive absolutely nothing, breathe slowly. Your own desire to receive messages may be blocking you. This can happen when you are preoccupied with successfully receiving insights. That's your ego showing up. It may also be that your partner is unconsciously blocking the connection. I've had clients who do this without even knowing it. I'll often sense an invisible wall. If this is the case, befriend the wall and engage with it. Perhaps invite it to express its reason for blocking information. Honor its presence and wisdom with kindness and compassion. Remain in this space for as long as you wish. Welcome the waves of insights that flow through you.

When you are ready to end this practice, take a few centering breaths with your partner and return your attention to your body. You are now ready to share the transmissions with your partner. Be sure to ask for permission first. This is your way of respecting their soul journey. As a general rule, messages should be expressed in a positive or neutral tone. Be very mindful of translating cautionary insights into messages that do not instill fear. Words carry frequency. Your choice of words and how you communicate matters. Remember your original intention of welcoming messages of Light and Love. Invite your partner to share their experience with you. What was their felt sense of the practice? They may have received intuitive messages for you as well.

Once you are both ready to end this session, join your palms together in a gesture of gratitude. You can say a few words thanking the Light for its loving presence.

STEP 4. TRUST. TRUST. TRUST.

Accelerating your intuition is a radical act of trusting the unseen. It's about "un-minding" the mind and peeling away the layers that control the ego's narratives. Trust is all about recalibrating the ego's perceived power. My greatest advice to you is simply to get out of your own way. Sounds simple, right? The ego often judges, questions, and distrusts. It's just doing its job. Acknowledge your ego without letting it take control. This is one of the biggest hurdles that we encounter on our intuitive path.

Your imagination is as real as the eyes reading these words. It operates in the unseen world. By trusting it, you gain access to deeper knowledge and cultivate a connection to Source. Become curious. Welcome new ideas. Invite your soul's essence to take up space. Watch synchronicities and coincidences abound. And ultimately radiate more Light.

In sessions with clients, I often feel like a time traveler who has been dropped onto a movie set. At other times, messages are presented as metaphors. The more I trust, the more comes through. For example, during an akashic reading for a friend, I saw an anthill swarming with ants. There was a sense of purposeful activity in this visual. I stayed with the energy of this image to receive more information. What came through was a metaphor for my friend's future participation with a network of lightworkers dedicated to raising humanity's vibration. The ants represented a very active online community.

STEP 5. CONNECT TO UNIVERSAL KNOWING

The previous four steps helped you set up a strong foundation. You're strengthening your intuitive listening skills, clearing and cleansing, committing to a regular meditation practice and trusting yourself. These are huge accomplishments. Think of all this as an ongoing lifelong process. The beauty of this journey is that it has no end point. The journey is the destination. I love the fact that I'm constantly evolving and receiving downloads. The more I know, the more I realize how much I don't know. Every day offers new experiences and new opportunities for growth. Your intuition is like a muscle and the more you develop it, the stronger it becomes. Like the old saying says: "Practice makes perfect".

Your connection to Source is a conduit for your intuition. You are a vessel of light visiting the library of infinite knowing. Repeat the practices and meditations from the previous chapters as often as you like. Notice how, every time, new insights further expand your awareness and confidence.

MEDITATION TO CONNECT TO SOURCE AND GAIN INSIGHTS

In this meditation, your intention is to attune to the frequency of Source. You will project your plasma into the ethers and bathe in the Light of Oneness. You'll need writing material. Remember the skills you've developed so far:

Grounding with 10 natural breaths

Setting an intention of light and love

Protecting yourself with this intention

Tuning in energetically to the higher dimensions

Connecting to Source

Listening intuitively, noticing sensations and trusting yourself

Sealing the experience with gratitude

Sit comfortably in your sacred space. Include a ritual such as lighting a candle if you are inspired to do so. Write down a question or inquiry. It's important that it be handwritten to alchemize its frequency. Breathe slowly and transition to a state of receptivity. Repeat the question a few times out loud. Let the spoken words imprint the space around you.

Begin meditating on your question with loving detachment. Release any attachment to a pre-determined answer and remain in a state of openness for at least 5 minutes. Notice if you begin to feel a shift in your overall energy. Perhaps it's your frequency amplifying. Maybe it's a guide coming through. Pay attention to any images, symbols, thoughts, emotions and sounds. This is most likely how your inquiry will be addressed. If needed, once you begin to receive downloads, ask for more details and clarification. Be still and wait. Again, notice what arises. You are in natural communion with universal knowing. Enjoy the beauty of this blessed moment. There's no need to rush. Linger for as long as you wish.

Once you are done, return to your breath awareness. Feel gratitude for the blessings of this experience. You may want to start journaling and continue receiving insights.

PRACTICE

Are there areas of your intuitive journey that you struggle with? Perhaps you have difficulty trusting yourself. Maybe you are uncomfortable with sitting quietly in meditation. Some of you may feel unworthy of your innate gifts. These are a few examples of struggles that can be encountered on your intuitive path.

In this practice, you'll explore blockages that can hold you back from fully accessing your intuition. Blockages play a vital role in your life, they act as protectors and gatekeepers. However, they can also hinder your development. You're invited to delve into your personal blocks and appreciate the wonderful opportunity they present for your expansion. What are you ready to release?

Take a few moments to contemplate your personal blocks. You may want to write them down and pay special attention to the words you have chosen. View them as living energy and encourage them to communicate with you. What emotions are coming up for you to tend to? Meditate on this. They may share old wounds or stories from your past that are ready to be lovingly released. You are peeling the layers that protect your heart. Be compassionate, patient and forgiving. You are clearing and opening up. The more clearing is done, the more is revealed for loving attention. And the more your intuitive gifts expand. You are clearing and opening up. The more clearing is done, the more is revealed for loving attention. And the more your intuitive gifts expand. This practice may take a few days, weeks or even years. For me, it's a daily practice.

STEP 6. A STATE OF CONSCIOUSNESS

When you infuse intuition into the connective tissue of your daily life, you start living from your heart center. You move closer and closer to your essence, the perfect geometry of your soul. This blessing dramatically enhances your soul journey. You truly embody the spirit of divine expression. Difficulties are alchemized into teaching moments and there is an appreciation for the generous blessings of life. This last step on your intuitive path encourages you to recognize your intuition as a sacred gift. It's your divine right.

The 2020 pandemic triggered traumatic memories in me. Like so many, I was gripped with fear, anxiety and grief. I relived the full spectrum of emotions from my bout with cancer 10 years prior. I realized that I was trying to hold everything together in a time of utter chaos. My emotional stability was unravelling before my eyes. I was a hot mess. In meditation, one of the core messages that came through was to seek stillness and bear witness to the full range of emotions presenting themselves. This was very challenging. Could I be in dialog with my fears? Could I become the observer and remain fully present? Essentially, the pandemic forced me to revisit unhealed trauma and deeply rooted fears. It enriched my spiritual practice.

During that chaotic year, a shift in consciousness occurred within me. There was an increased level of authenticity in my practices born from my vulnerability. It was a new level of awakening to Truth and its unwavering still point. In moments of darkness, its light imbued me with love. I just needed to return to this sacred sanctuary, time and time again. During my long walks in nature, I observed how the trees remained tree-like, unaware and unaffected by the world changes. This in itself was a revelation. Could I be like the trees?

We are ascending towards a new paradigm. The spiritual alarm clock has rung. It's time to awaken humanity. Can we transcend this matrix and manifest a world founded on the principles of loving kindness? How will we get there?

FUTURE SELF MEDITATION

Settle comfortably into your sacred space. Begin to breathe mindfully. Set an intention that only energies of light and love be present. Count 10 breaths.

Begin to drop deeper into your body. Befriend stillness. Feel the special-ness of this moment. Experience its spaciousness. Notice any sensations in your body.

In your mind's eye, visualize yourself standing in front of two very large ancient wooden doors. Notice their texture, height, width and any other details. Walk up to the doors. Open them and step onto a scene from your future life. Notice the environment you have entered into. Become aware of sounds, smells, people, geographic location, time of day, and any other details you sense. Be curious. Walk around freely. What do you see? Spend time here to fully explore this experience.

Now delve deeper into the details. What more do you see, feel, smell, sense? What is your future self doing? Can you talk to your future self? Begin a dialog with her/him. Ask as many questions as you want. Share ideas and thoughts. How is your present self different from your future one? Be grateful for the insights you receive.

When you are ready to return to your current reality, focus your attention on your breath. Give yourself permission to fully integrate the essence of your experience into the present moment. Come to a seated position. Join your palms together in a gesture of gratitude. Thank your higher guidance for the blessings of this meditation.

You may want to journal on this experience.

EMERGING

Do you sense a shift occurring within you? Are things not quite as they seem? When you observe yourself, do you feel a subtle knowing that something is preparing to manifest? Are you being called to be of service in some way? Are you ready to step into a new expression of yourself? What is your unique talent and how can you share it with your community to raise the collective vibration? So many questions to explore!

Emerging is a lifelong process of shedding, releasing and shifting into new timelines. Like the proverbial caterpillar that transforms into a butterfly, we are constantly activating new versions of ourselves. There can be moments of joy and anticipation as well as confusion, anxiety and grief. You may feel as though at times you are taking 2 steps forward and 3 steps back. View this dance as a gift. You are actually cleansing at a deep level by peeling the layers of old wounds and memories. Invoke the healing energy of forgiveness and love, especially towards yourself. Be compassionate. In my personal journey, the more layers I peel away, the more that is revealed to heal.

A new multi-dimensional human is emerging on this planet. This human is tapping into his/her crystalline energy body and awakening to a new paradigm. You are most likely one of these. The fact that you are reading this book and tuning into its messages is an indication that something is emerging from within you. You intuitively know that your DNA codes are being activated to raise your frequency and access higher dimensions. Welcome these blessings.

During the 2020 pandemic, I experienced a huge energetic shift. There was anxiety, sadness, fear and anger. In many ways, I felt helpless. There was also curiosity, love and compassion. I witnessed the level of panic that gripped the planet. This massive worldwide event shook many of us to our core. I knew that something momentus was emerging in the collective consciousness. Humanity was being challenged in every way. I experienced a rising awareness of our innate potential for co-creating out of chaos. There was a desire to return to simplicity and truth, to embrace the divine expression of our soul's blueprint. People connected on new platforms. We are birthing a new human expression.

The more time I spent in nature seeking stillness, meditating and raising my vibration, the more I accessed internal light codes. I began to tap into universal Truth, humbled by its magnitude. It felt expansive and light. A discernible shift was taking place. I toggled between 2 worlds, the 3D reality and the realms of 5D. I sought time alone to connect with the incoming higher frequencies that were piercing through the chaos. Back in 3D reality, I was able to bear witness to events, relationships and people with a new perspective. This facilitated an editing process in areas of my life that were ready to be cleared. It included parts of myself that no longer resonated with what was emerging. It was and continues to be a messy and necessary process.

EMERGING PRACTICE

Stand or sit comfortably in front of a mirror. Count 10 natural breaths. With each breath, have a sense of your body settling into a state of relaxation. Once you feel grounded, gaze at yourself and focus on your eyes. Maintain a steady gaze. Place your right palm on your heart center. Let it receive the warmth of your palm. Invite your heart to communicate with you. Notice what you are feeling. What do the eyes behind your eyes see? Infuse this experience with the presence of your divine nature and send yourself beams of loving energy.

Begin an authentic dialog with your heart and soul. Notice if your mind wants to contribute to the conversation. Acknowledge your ego then return to your focus. What is wanting to manifest from deep within? What is emerging? What is arising for you to tend to? What is ready to be cleared?

The following questions can assist in this exploration:

Do you feel a shift emerging from within you like a heartfelt desire for change?

Describe the felt sensation around this shift?

Can you transform this desire into an intention?

What do you really want for your life?

What ignites you?

How do you see yourself one year from now? Describe your vision in detail.

During this practice, maintain a steady gaze. You may even drop down deeper into your inner heart to expand your practice. Welcome more loving messages.

Tell yourself 3 times out loud that you love yourself. Bathe in this affirmation. To seal this contemplation, return to your breath. Start a journal to record your thoughts and insights. Repeat this practice as often as you like. Surprise yourself with new insights and ideas.

MANIFESTING MEDITATION

Settle comfortably into your sacred space. Make sure that you are undisturbed for the duration of the meditation. Begin breathing mindfully. Gently slow down your inhales and extend your exhales without forcing anything. Count 10 breaths.Set an intention that only energies of Light and Love are welcome for your highest good.

Shift your awareness to your body and feel it relaxing completely. Now settle your awareness on the center point inside your skull. Visualize your pineal gland, also known as the seat of your soul. Intuitively sense its location in the center of your head. The pineal gland is associated with your 3rd eye and your imagination. Inner vision, insight and high intelligence are alchemized here. The pineal gland is an invaluable tool for creating your reality by projecting images into the ethers. As you rest your awareness on this incredible manifesting tool, recognize your capacity to shift into a heightened reality. Begin to visualize what you want to manifest in your 3D reality. Take your time to see it in as much detail as you can.

Project this hologram into the ethers from your pineal gland. Feel its magnetic resonance transforming the matrix of your reality. Now release your attachment to the visual. Give it the space and time to manifest at the right moment in the right place for your highest good.

Return to your breath. Move your fingers and toes. You may want to stretch as well. If you are lying down, come up to a seated position. Join your palms together. Let your thumbs rest on your heart center and lower your chin toward your chest to seal this meditation with love and gratitude. Surround it with it love.

Stay here for as long as you wish. Allow the blessings of this meditation to infuse every cell of your body with their light.

FAILURE

All my actions, thoughts

and mistakes

have led me

to this blessed moment.

We often hear the expression "Failure is not an option" Wow! Feel into the unyielding quality of this statement. Not only is failure an option, it's a necessity for our growth. What if we changed our narrow lens and viewed failure as an incredible teaching opportunity? What would that look like?

Failure is the expression of an unfulfilled intention. We judge an outcome as successful or not based on a particular objective. Failure can be disappointing, embarrassing and shameful. We've been programmed to compete against one another, to outdo the opponent, to be #1. This breeds division, separation and isolation. Losers are often ridiculed and rejected. Just look at our corporate and educational systems, the sports complex, the entertainment industry and organizations. Let's be honest, competition is healthy and necessary at times. It can bring out the best in us. The question however is, at what cost? What if we altered our view of the outcome? What if grace, insight, wisdom and forgiveness were integral to the intention? Imagine what our world would look like. Our emotional intelligence and spiritual growth would expand in ways we can't even begin to imagine. Society as we know it would experience a quantum leap. I believe that we are on the cusp of this. Our true power will no longer emanate from unhealthy competitive values, but rather from humans helping each other grow. Rather than promoting survival of the fittest, we will celebrate a thriving human collective.

I've personally failed at many ventures and projects. At times the financial results were dismal. Yet the personal growth for both myself and others was immeasurable. More often than not, I had to reconsider my definition of success. It's only in the past few years that I finally view my past as a succession of extraordinary teaching moments. I invite you to do the same. Revisit your "failures" and see them as brilliant offerings of self-discovery. How did you emerge from them? What were the learnings? It's time to rewrite your story and change the narrative.

PRACTICE: REWRITE YOUR STORY

Contemplate areas in your life where you have judged an experience as a failure. This could be a relationship, an endeavor, a project or an unfulfilled dream. Notice any sensations in your body as you play back these memories. What do you feel? Where are you feeling these emotions and sensations? Observe if you are judging yourself.

Select one of these experiences for this practice. Begin by releasing your attachment to the word failure and its influence on your subconscious. Tell yourself that this experience was not a failure. Instead, replace the word failure with learning. Use the following affirmation: "I was blessed with this event in my life so that I could learn and experience......" fill in the dots. Repeat 3 times out loud.

Let the acoustics of this new narrative imprint your field of consciousness. You are rescripting your past and clearing it. This is a powerful practice.

Now take the time to handwrite your new story. The act of writing is key to changing neuro pathways of the brain and reprogramming your mind. You are actually creating a new reality. Tape this handwritten affirmation onto a mirror,and stand in front of it. Read your affirmation three times out loud again while looking at yourself. Do this for 7 days.

Go back to other events in your life which you'd like to clear and repeat this practice. Welcome insights.

FORGIVENESS MEDITATION

Sit up comfortably in your sacred space. Make sure that you are undisturbed for the duration of your meditation. Begin breathing mindfully. Count 10 breaths.

This meditation will invite you to place your right palm in different positions and repeat a blessing 3 times, either out loud or to yourself. Allow time for integration between each blessing.

Shift your awareness to your body and feel it relaxing completely.

1. Place your right palm on your lower belly. Repeat the following mantra 3 times: "I honor and bless my inner wisdom." Remain still for 1 minute.

2. Place your right palm on your middle belly, around the navel area. Repeat the following mantra 3 times: "I honor and bless the teacher within me." Remain still for 1 minute.

3. Place your right palm on your heart center. Repeat the following mantra 3 times: "I honor and bless my heart. I love myself unconditionally." Remain still for 1 minute.

4. Place your right palm on your left shoulder, by your neck. Repeat the following mantra 3 times: "I honor and bless the power within me to release myself of guilt." Remain still for 1 minute.

5. Place your right palm across your forehead. Repeat the following mantra 3 times: "I honor and bless my capacity to forgive others. I choose to forgive and release my attachment to past wounds." Remain still for 1 minute.

6. Place your right palm behind hour head. Repeat the following mantra 3 times: "I honor and bless my capacity to forgive myself.

I choose to forgive myself. I choose to love myself unconditionally." Remain still for 1 minute.

7. Place your right palm approximately 4 inches above your head. Repeat the following mantra 3 times: " I honor and bless my Self. I honor and bless my Higher Self." Remain still for 1 minute.

Sit in stillness for a few minutes to fully absorb the harmonics of this meditation at a cellular level. When you are ready to seal this blessing, join your palms together in gratitude.

I once taught this meditation at a men's correctional center. At the end of the class, an inmate came up to me. He told me that for the first time in his life, he was able to contemplate the possibility of forgiveness. He was serving a life sentence and had already been there for 20 years. The meditation had unlocked something within him. He realized that he held the power of forgiveness within him. I was blessed with the grace of that moment and knew that this meditation had triggered a profound shift in him. I also sensed that Source had been channeled in that class.

INTUITIVE OFFERINGS

In meditation, I often receive messages from Light Beings as offerings of wisdom and love. In the following channeled transmissions, I invite you to experience their inspirational words.

THE GROUP OF LIGHT BEINGS

This galactic group has a masculine resonance. They wear long unadorned robes and seem to levitate a few inches off the ground. Their leader greets me with the following words: "We are here now".

He then presents me with a vintage microphone. It's both a metaphor and invitation for me to be their microphone. I accept and ask: "What is the message?"

He answers with one word: "Healer"

He adds that each human is a powerful healer. We hold these keys in our DNA and our connection to Source. We access healing through the photonic patterns of our divine light. He adds that humanity is on the cusp of activating and receiving new healing harmonics on planet earth. There are symphonies of new light frequencies cascading upon the earth plane to activate these codes.

"How will we experience this new energy?" I ask.

He answers: "Love frequency."

Love will become the new currency on this planet. Love heals spirit. Love activates ascension. We are crossing into a new paradigm and have had to detoxify on every level. They invite me to dive deeper into this concept. I am encouraged to contemplate difficulties in our lives such as illness, death, separation, tragedy and suffering. We are to inquire: "What is the healing opportunity in this situation?" With the magnetic resonance of pure love, the answers are readily available. Love opens the portals to the gift that has presented itself. You may think this idea is simplistic, almost childlike. You are right, truth is simple. This is how the Group of Light Beings transmits multi-vibrational information. This technique is integral to their galactic technology. Your frequency is shifting as you read these words.

I've survived cancer and numerous challenges in my life. Love was not my first response to these events. Quite the opposite. I experienced fear, anxiety, anger, depression and grief. In 2010, my family moved to the United States from Canada for a job opportunity. That year was intense. I worked and travelled extensively in a stressful yet highly energizing environment. The following year, after a routine test, I was diagnosed with cancer. Within 3 days of these test results, I was thrown into a world of biopsies, surgery, intense chemotherapy, radiation and all the emotional trauma associated with cancer treatment. My world had completely collapsed. I recall a turning point when I consciously decided to begin a dialog with the cancer. I called it "the visitor". Rather than fight it, I invited the visitor to help me better understand. What was its purpose or message? In meditation, I infused my body with healing love and included this visitor in my intention. I also refused to say the word cancer, because it triggered severe anxiety in me. That year was exceptionally challenging. I feared death and leaving behind my young daughter and husband. I struggled with my identity. There were many days of depression. It often felt like a dark and heavy cauldron. I was at the bottom of it. In meditation, I could sink to that place. As my meditation deepened, I would move out through its wall and into a new space. Here there was stillness and light. It was the expansive quality of universal love, always present. Love held the vessel. Love gave me permission to be angry, sad, afraid and helpless. It took many years to process the experience of this illness.

The group of Light Beings returns. They transmit one word:

42

"ASCENSION." I am infused with Truth, Love and Light. One of the Group members raises both his arms horizontally to communicate that the ascension process is not necessarily a vertical upward movement, but rather an expansive process. We tend to think of ascension in a hierarchical way. Our 3D reality is an access point, a portal. It's as richly rewarding as the higher dimensions. Everything is interconnected. The process of awakening is a fully integrated experience.

THE NATIVE INDIAN GODDESS

She appears with magnificent white feathered wings that extend 10 feet out. In one sweeping transformation, she then shapeshifts into a larger than life native Indian goddess dressed in stunning ceremonial attire. Her splendor is powerful. She asks me: "Are you living your Divinity?" She encourages me to meditate on this oracle. Can I immerse my divine Self into my physical reality and truly live a fully embodied life? What a magical message of love.

THE SHAMAN

A wise old Shaman appears. He's like a lovable absent-minded professor, a little disheveled and quirky. At times, he seems somewhat embarrassed. He struggles with finding adequate words to fully express the depth of what he wants to impart. He sits next to me in his long robe and draws my attention to his hands. He touches my cheek with one hand and shares one word: TOUCH. He wants me to recognize the incredible power of this blessing. Touch carries vibration and frequency. It is sacred medicine, an important human technology. Many humans do not know this. Touch can communicate, heal, receive and love. He conveys another word: CURIOSITY. I interpret this as an invitation to be curious. He then follows up with another word: SILENCE. He wants me to practice more stillness. To speak less. The more silent I become, the more connected I am to Source. I feel more tuned in. I welcome curiosity. There is clarity. There is knowing.

I am then overwhelmed with the light filled appearance of a younger man. His name is Jesus. He reveals that the cancer I experienced was a passage, not a test. He underlines this word, PASSAGE. He adds: "You will find me in places you least expect to". My intuition guides me to further explore this cryptic statement. What comes up is that he is influencing world leaders in a worldwide shift. He is facilitating a galactic convergence of humans.

TWO DOORS

Two large translucent glass doors appear in meditation. They are tall, sleek and slightly ajar. Brilliant light streams through the opening between them. I receive a telepathic download that the light is a metaphor for the 5th dimension. In order to access this dimension, we have to transform ourselves to fit through their narrow opening. The doors will not open any wider. The onus is on us to do the work. How? By altering our frequency. There are many ways of doing this. Practices such as meditation, mindfulness, loving kindness, compassion, being of service, living our dharma and nature walks are just a few examples of how we can accelerate this process. These practices have an amplifying and cleansing effect on our plasma field. They enhance the transition to these realms. When we live from the embodied 5D dimension, our 3D reality here on earth takes on a whole new meaning. There is a natural knowing that permeates everything. We understand the nature of energy. We feel connected to Source and experience grace even during challenging times.

PRACTICE TRANSMUTING ENERGY

The following self-inquiry invites you to shift your perspective on a personal challenge you are experiencing. Try to hand write the answers to anchor them in 3D:

Is there a part of your life that you are struggling with?

Describe the energy around it?

What do you feel emotionally?

What do you feel physically?

Now shift into viewing this situation as a teaching moment......

List the learnings that you are experiencing from this situation?

For example: self-love, patience, discipline, sovereignty, independence, peace, empathy, presence, kindness, forgiveness, change, intuitive awakening, etc

What emotions are associated to these learnings?

How does your energy feel when you explore these emotions?

Do you feel there is still more to learn from this challenging situation?

MEDITATION ON THE "I AM"

This meditation includes a mantra. If you practice rituals to bless your space, do so now. Sit comfortably on a pillow or chair. Ideally, you should be in an upright position. Begin to breathe mindfully. Slow down the inhales and extend the exhales without forcing anything. Breath should move naturally in and out. Count up to 10 breaths.

Drop deeper into your body. Befriend stillness. Feel the specialness of this moment. Experience its spaciousness. Notice any sensations in your body.

Place your right palm on your heart center and your left one on your lower belly. Feel your heart and belly receiving the warmth of your palms. Set an intention that this meditation be filled with love and light. Rest your awareness on your crown chakra, located a few inches above your head. Breathe into this space.

Repeat the following "I AM" mantra 3 times out loud to imprint your energy field with the harmonics of the words.

I Am Universal Love

This Little Book of Offerings

I Am Divine Light

I Am attuned to the Perfect Geometry of All that Is

I Am Well

And so it is

And so it is.

Remain here for however long feels right. Allow time for your heart center to express itself with love. Experience new insights and guidance.

Seal this practice with gratitude by bringing your palms together and lowering your head towards your heart as a gesture of reverence for its blessing.

YOU ARE A GALACTIC CITIZEN

This book of offerings was co-created with the group of Light Beings. Their message is clear. We are not helpless souls stuck in a limited 3D matrix. Quite the contrary. We are so much more than that. We are all interconnected and empowered divine beings living an embodied experience. We are millions and millions of facets of an ever expanding alchemical grid.

We are all essentially galactic beings. Our home at this time just happens to be planet earth. There are trillions of other planets and galaxies out there, many of which are inhabited by other life forms. The stories we've been fed about UFOs and ETs are rife with subtle messages of fear, separation and distrust. Think of the programming we've received from the media, the entertainment industry, religion and culture. What if the universe was filled with beings of Light excited to co-create with us, their cosmic brothers and sisters?

We often refer to galactic beings as "higher dimensional entities". This hierarchal point of view positions humans as "lower beings." Within our DNA codes however, we hold the keys to unlocking our supernatural potential. Also known as "junk" DNA, these codes hold the power of the newly awakened inter planetary citizen. That's you, dear One! This means that you have the opportunity to embrace your incredible superpower as a Being of Light and ascend to new heights of consciousness. Immerse yourself in this powerful message. Feel every divine cell in your body awakening to the magnitude of this transmission. Breathe it in.

For many humans, the process of ascension is happening right now. Many of us are moving into a new consciousness. We are experiencing a radical shift. This is an internal activation of the hidden codes within each one of us. My guides have expressed a strong desire to assist us. Simply call on them and feel their presence.

Now is the time to do the internal clearing and cleansing work. Not only is the Earth's resonance rising, so is ours. I am convinced that in the coming years we will connect with our cosmic family in a much more public spirit of collaboration and kinship. Imagine learning new technologies from them and sharing our earthly wisdom. Imagine that!

You are a galactic citizen simply by the nature that you reside in a galaxy. You may even be a blend of multiple galactic beings, just like your ancestral lineage is made up of multiple races. You may feel compelled to research your galactic lineage. You may be a blend of star races.

We are ready to rediscover our true nature. This journey can be scary, energizing and expansive all at once. There is so much to process. It's ok to feel extreme emotions. Take exceptional care of yourself. We are releasing old paradigms and co-creating new ones. On my personal path, there have been days when I felt confused. And on other days, my entire being vibed with a new clarity, something incredibly powerful. That's why it's important to practice self-care and to be kind to yourself. I've shared numerous practices in this book to assist you in navigating energetic shifts.

MEDITATION TO CONNECT TO YOUR GUIDES
Find a comfortable seat or lie back in your sacred space. If you practice rituals to ground your energy, go ahead and do so prior to settling down. You may want to light a candle, set up crystals around you, play soft music, chant a mantra or diffuse essential oils for example. Whatever inspires you.

Begin breathing mindfully, through your nostrils if that feels comfortable. Observe the gentle ebb and flow of your breath. Drop in deeper with 10 breaths. Feel your body becoming relaxed. Set an intention that only energies of Light and Love may enter your energy field.

Choose one of the following intentions and repeat it 3 times out loud or silently. You are broadcasting your permission to your guides for them to communicate with you:

1. "I call on my highest level guides in Light and Love to guide me with a particular situation. Let this be for my greatest good."

2. "I call on my highest level guides in Light and Love to share loving messages and help me expand so that I may be of greater service to my human family. Let this be for my greatest good."

3. "I call on my highest level guides in Light and Love to be in open dialog with me. Let this be for my greatest good."

Remain in your field of consciousness. Feel spacious and open. Notice subtle shifts within and around you. Try not to have any expectations, especially with timing. This process can take time. You are outside of linear time. What may seem like 5 minutes in your reality, may actually end up being much longer and vice versa. This is normal when you are in a higher state of consciousness.

Notice whatever comes through. When you feel your guides' presence, pay special attention to their unique energetic frequency. They may be galactic friends, deceased relatives, native spirits, animals, angels, ascended masters or fairies for example. Guides often express themselves through felt sensation, emotion, symbols, sounds, colors and images. If you're uncertain and want more clarity, it's perfectly ok to ask for details. Be curious. If at any time you feel uncomfortable, remember that you are in control. You can stop at any time.

The 3 tenants of this process are:

1. LISTEN with your heart

2. TRUST whatever is coming through

3. TRANSLATE the language of your guides

If you are not receiving anything, don't judge yourself. Take this time to fully enjoy your meditation. Messages from your guides may manifest at a later time, or in another meditation. You may be putting too much pressure on yourself and blocking the channel. Notice if this is the case. Do not judge yourself. Relax and return to your intention. The more you are relaxed and at ease, the greater the chances of connection.

When you have completed this meditation, seal it with an empowering intention. Here is a suggestion which you can say out loud or to yourself: " I am ready to claim my divine power. To live my highest potential. And so it is."

In closing, thank your guides for their presence and loving kindness. This is important. They will appreciate your gratitude. Take a few deep breaths to return to your physical reality.

This meditation can be repeated as many times as you like. You may notice that as you become more comfortable with it and dive deeper, the communications with your guides become more immediate and direct.

PRACTICE INTUITIVE JOURNALING

Start a personal journal. Begin to write down transmissions from your meditations. You can also add intuitive writing to the process by writing freely with your non-dominant hand. This allows your soul to express itself without filters. Stay with your heart's wisdom. Enjoy the process and any messages that come through.

You may even feel compelled to start a small spiritual group to meditate in community and share your experiences. There is great power in group energy. I highly recommend that if you decide to start a group, you practice extreme discernment in regards to who you allow in. This is not an elitist statement but rather an intention to honor the integrity of the group's energy.

BLANK CANVAS

This book was written intuitively. I trusted the guidance that co-created each offering with me. My intention was to express the purity and simplicity of the messages without judgement.

I now invite you to write your own high vibe offerings and share them with the world. You are unique and very creative. Your potential is limitless. Let your crystalline energy radiate and warm the hearts of those blessed to encounter you on their path.

Simply begin with a blank page and see what comes through......

Blessings.